# Business Is Business

## COACHING AND AFFIRMATIONS TO ACHIEVE BUSINESS GOALS

### R. SHELTON, MBA

# Dedication

When I was young, I would go to my grandmother's, and in the mornings, I would wake up to the smell of coffee, grits, and eggs. Till this day I remember seeing her sitting at the table reading her bible and sipping her coffee and she would say with a soft musical tone, "here she comes Miss America." I would smile from ear to ear because those simple words always made me feel like I could conquer the world. Ok, so maybe I was only Miss America in my mind, but because of her, I knew I could do anything. Dedicating this book to people who are not afraid to grow, not afraid to jump, and not afraid to win.

Love you always, Granny.

# Table of Contents

Introduction ................................................. 4-5

Chapter 1 ................................................ 6-16

Chapter 2 ............................................... 17-23

Chapter 3 ............................................... 24-28

Chapter 4 ............................................... 29-32

Chapter 5 ............................................... 33-36

Chapter 6 ............................................... 37-41

Chapter 7 ............................................... 42-48

Daily Affirmations ................................... 46-51

Recap ..................................................... 52-54

# Introduction

In today's society business is the embodiment of a person's ability to earn a living and leave a mark on society. In everyday life, we fail to look at how the word business can be incorporated into everything we do. When we make appointments, have conferences, or plan personal events we are engaging in business transactions. When we step back and look at our overall life, we participate in business transactions twenty-four hours a day, seven days a week. Life can be even more stressful when you also run a company, have a career or are trying to plan for a future. Whether you are a homemaker, entrepreneur, or work in an office, you can use coaching on how to manage the business of life and the businesses you create to earn a living.

## Who:

This book is for small business owners looking to take their business to the next level

This book will help you enlarge your coast

This book is for the individual seeking to advance into new positions and find out where they want to be in their career

This book is for your day-to-day planning and goals

## How:

How to plan day to day for future growth

How to brainstorm through socializing and networking

How to market your business or you

How to set goals and give yourself positive affirmations

## Why:

You need this book because you are struggling with certain aspects of your business, and you don't know how to get out of the rut.

You need more income to maintain your business, lifestyle, and household

You need business strategies that help you grow into an actual CEO and not a worker

You need better customer or client interaction

You need structure

## What:

The book can impact you at any level in your career or business development

The book will show you how to apply the skills you need to grow

Each chapter will allow you to engage in conversation or thought

The book encourages self-encouragement


This book is for YOU!


Now head on over to Chapter 1.

# CHAPTER ONE

*"The better we manage for the business of life, the better our lives will be when we are managing business!"*

# Chapter 1 – The Assessment

So, you want to be a boss. What is a Boss? A B.O.S.S is a **B**randed **O**rganized **S**ustainable **S**pirit. That functions through strategy and proper planning. First, you build a brand through an organized path. Then you show evident sustainability by proving you have staying power. Lastly, you have the spirit of a leader. In other words, everything you do is done in decency and order. Many times, people confuse dictating, pointing fingers, and controlling with the idea of being a boss. You do not have to control others or put them beneath you to accomplish a task or goal. If you possess the right qualities and have accessed your personal growth needs, you can operate with the essence of a B.O.S.S. in all areas of your life and business.

**Let's assess your current business qualities**

Now, what are you currently doing right and what are you currently doing wrong? Having deficiencies in your business practices is not the end. It does not mean you are a horrible business owner, but once you recognize the issues its imperative to put plans in place to correct the deficiencies. The best way to approach this is by taking inventory of your rights and wrongs. Make a list of everything in your business and personal life that is going well and everything that needs help. The reason you want to look at business and personal is that your personal affairs will often spill over into your work life or business. Taking a self-assessment is just as important as a business assessment. A personal assessment also lets you be in control of how you improve without the backlash of customers, clients, and employers prompting the assessment.

*I am determined to be the best me!*

### What about you and your business is unique?

Once you have made a list of all the good things you have going for you, decide which things are unique to only your business. From a more personal perspective take a long look at you and determine what about you is unique and different from everyone else. If you cannot find one thing unique about how you work, the services you offer, or how you run your business, then this is your first project. Your first project is to create something unique and exclusive to you, something that people must come to you for, or people remember you for. There may be thousands of beauty salons or barbershops in your area, but what do you offer that stands out to your customer. When you consider every major company in America or even the world, there is something unique about each of them that you cannot find anywhere else.

*In my uniqueness, I will rise above my competition!*

### In what areas of your business can you do better?

Now that we have decided what makes you unique and in what areas you perform well. Lets' look at the not so good side of business and life. Are you failing yourself in promoting and marketing? Do you need better supplies or to reorganize your business tools? When you look at your personal life are you separating your home problems from your business? Is your business legitimate or are you missing certain licenses or credentials? Are you faking it till you make it? These are the questions you should be asking yourself. Once you identify the issues, you can begin to fix them. As the old saying goes, "once you admit you have a problem, that's the first step."

In the scheme of things, you know what you have to offer, and you know how you want to do it. Are you checking inventory on your practices and fixing the issues? Remember this is your vision coming to fruition, and you must take inventory often to keep everything on track towards your goals. When you run out of milk, you buy more, so when you run out of steam or ideas, you must restock. Now some of you may be reading this and saying I am just looking for a career! Well, you also need to assess your good and bad qualities. This should be the first thing you do when you don't see yourself or your business growing. Begin now to envision your success and determine how to get there. So together let's plan and strategize to reach your goals.

*I can do better, each day I will look at myself and work on fixing my issues.*

**Are you getting the money you deserve?**

Money is always at the top of most people's radar. How can I get the most of this opportunity? Determining your worth can be easy for some and hard for others. Many things factor into what you get in compensation for services and from a career. Cost of living can play a huge role in what you charge, where you work and what you get paid. It also determines what companies, positions, and services strive in your area. There are instances where you can be the determining factor to how well something will do, or you may have to change your surroundings to make a career choice or business venture work. The remarkable thing going for most of us currently is the Internet. Online forums and sites now let you compare salaries, create an ad, and more. The internet also allows you to be anywhere in the world and conduct business on a global and international level. You can interact by video chat or live stream with a broad audience. The internet makes going global easier than ever. The goal in any business venture is to grow, so expansion is vital. The key to increasing your income, developing your brand, and securing your presence in the future is having the right tools at your disposal.

You also must consider your why? In business, you do it because it is something you love or something you need. Either way being financially secure is the end goal. Many of us spend years in college and thousands of dollars on learning new skills only to be in the same position. Normally after ending one chapter of learning, we want to apply what we learned and start making the big bucks, but how many people finish school and still have no real plan or colossal career offers? Yes, a whole lot of people. The question becomes did you choose the right course of study and are you engaging in your purpose. Do not get stuck focusing on one life experience. Be willing to explore who you are and turn it into a career.

Like our current generation says how will you "secure the bag." That is youthful talk for how you will bring in the money just in case anyone was lost. As entrepreneur's who do not have an external product to offer, this can be a difficult area because you are your product. Sometimes convincing people of your worth is extremely hard and even harder to prove to yourself. You must spend more time building your brand and creating opportunities. Getting yourself known is better than the initial money you will bring in, so focus on becoming a household name. There will always be others with the same trade or services you offer, but keep in mind quality wins over price. The idea is to stay in business to compete so do not let overconfidence kill your drive and will to succeed. The money you deserve will come so do not let the fear of not getting what you are worth stand in the way of learning, listening, and growing.

*A slack hand causes poverty, but the hand of the diligent makes rich.*

*Proverbs ESV 10:4*

**Avoiding Poverty and Embracing Richness**

In everything we do, there is a word to support you. We must be willing to listen to hear our purpose and the instructions to achieve our goals. The bible may not be the first book we all turn to, but it is full of life lessons and how to avoid being poor is one of them. Let's take this Proverb for example and use it as a business tool. If you have set a mission statement for your business, it should be focused on how to avoid SLACK. When we consider people, who live with a slack hand, meaning they are lazy and unproductive. They often live in poverty and poverty is a result of slack. When we fail to move in any aspect of our lives especially in careers and business opportunities, we create a spirit of poverty. It doesn't mean you have nothing; it says you are not meeting your full potential.

**Slow-fulness**

**Loose**

**Attitude**

**Careless**

**Kinship**

When a person possesses a **slow-fulness**, it's draining to every aspect of business and life in general. Things get put off day after day until ultimately nothing is accomplished year after year. This can develop into a slothful behavior or laziness.

**Loose** and **attitude** go together because when your attitude is loose or detached from reality, then you are easily taken to a place that is not productive for your business. Having a loose or dissolute attitude about your work ethic leaves you vulnerable to poverty and unethical behavior. This is not good for business and can put you in situations that cause you to fail or even face criminal situations. Like tax fraud for example.

**Careless**, when you are careless in how you operate then you fail to put importance on anything. Ultimately you could care less about how things run and how people feel about your services. In business, we must have a servant heart but the mentality of a leader. Carelessness will leave you vulnerable to all kinds of mayhem.

Now **Kinship** is focused on what you pass on to those around you. When you establish a mindset of poverty, you pass it on from one generation to the next. When we look at generational poverty, it can be direct or indirect. It can also be genetic. Just because one parent is focused on business does not mean your children or those related to you will follow the same work ethic. Kinship also addresses those you associate with. We have all heard the phrase, "birds of feather flock together." This phrase shows you how strong kinship is and how just the people you associate with can either lift you up or bring you down to their poverty level.

The goal when you are venturing out in business is to teach and pass on the fundamentals and help your kin build as well. The flip side to this is also not allowing your kinship to drive your business in the ground. You never want to open your business up to kinfolk, friends or associates just because of your relationship ties. This is a sure way to cause your business to fail and ruin your relationships. You can lead a man or woman to water, but you cannot force them to drink. This means you can show people good business ethics and hard work, but you cannot force them to have the same work ethics that you need to push your business forward. They dehydrated in a sense. They are lacking the desire necessary to be hydrated with knowledge.

Now how do we avoid SLACK and focus on being RICH, according to the proverb we must be diligent in all that we do. Diligence is what brought you to seek knowledge and improve your business skills, so you are on the right path already. How does being RICH translate in your life?

**Ratified**

**Investments**

**Create**

**Heirs**

In real estate, an offer is not confirmed until it has been ratified. **Ratified** means making it official or valid. In any business transaction, you do not have an official deal until it has been ratified. An imaginary signature that says I accept this service, I am pleased with this service, and I will seek this service out again. Ratified merely equals satisfaction, and satisfaction equals more and more business. We want our clients and our employers to give us that official stamp of approval every time.

**Investment**, not only do you want others to invest in you, but you want to make the right investments when it comes to your assets, your time, and people. Investments require risk, you may lose a little, but the goal is to gain a lot. When we invest in ourselves, we see the most significant gain. Have you ever taken time out to get a pedicure or a haircut and felt good about yourself? Thru that you have gained a higher self-awareness. It makes you feel good. Imagine investing in your knowledge, investing in your personal growth, or investing in your business. All these investments lead you to higher profits and a feeling of accomplishment.

**Create**, to be rich, you must be diligent in all these areas, but you must create new ways to do business depending on market changes. Everyone will have a peak and off-peak moments in business, but what we create during these times is what separates one business from another. Learning what makes all your times; peak times, by creating a consistent need is what places you ahead of the competition. Focusing on your creative self will help you come up with new ways of doing business. People create something new every day so learning how to apply what others design is also key to your advancement.

Lastly, the goal should be to create heirs. **Heirs** are different from kinship because an heir has a sense of entitlement. When you create heirs, you mold and shape them to carry the torch. With business, your success is measured in part by those who can inherit it and continue to grow it. All the major companies we see today started small and were inherited time after time to become major brands and iconic symbols in our communities and the world. When we look at companies like Disney, McDonald's, or even Walmart we could not imagine a society without these major brands. A small vision in some one's mind grew into what we all know as our norm or what we see as a symbol of the American dream.

In addition to major brands being inherited in our society, when we look at our children and those, we care about we want to leave a legacy. We want those who inherit it to understand it, work with the same enthusiasm, and have the same diligence as we did to grow it. Many great businesses and ideas fizzle out with the person who created it because there is no one with the same drive and passion for carrying on after you are gone. Even in your careers how many of you are producing generational doctors, lawyers, and philanthropist. Take a long look at who will carry on your life's work and who you are building within the process. Now when I say who you are building with, I am talking about your significant other. There is a significant difference in building alone and building with your love partner. If the highest emotion in life is love, imagine the power a love bond can create when you build together.

      Building is significant to see your full potential and can only be done with those who lift you up. So never build with constructive criticism. Something designed to build you up should never follow up with tearing you down. Until you have a partner, seek mentorship. Mentorship is also an excellent way to create heirs when we don't have offspring or direct connections to continue our life's work. The lesson here is when we embrace the fullness of life, no matter our circumstances and diligently work towards our goals, we will live a rich and fulfilled life.

*I will embrace my desire to achieve a full and rich life!*

## CHAPTER TWO

*"Success depends upon previous preparation, and without such preparation, there is sure to be failure."*

*~ Confucius*

## Chapter 2- Strategize

Coming up with a strategy can make a huge difference in how you perform in any business realm. When a plan of action takes form, people take notice. By having a strategy, you find ways to increase income versus hoping your income magically goes up. Continually renewing yourself and adding new fresh ideas is a strategy. Using follow-up tools and feedback is a way to help you plan and strategize. Now lets' think of the word action. An action is a process of doing. If you are not doing something, then you will not move forward. Planning and action will move you forward with a solid foundation ahead of you.

**Create ways you can increase income**

Creativity can come natural to some people and hard to others. Research is always an excellent way to start. Think about what you want, are good at and then incorporate that into a way to increase your income. For example, if you are good at writing, then some ways to increase your income is to help others write resume's, start a blog, or become a ghostwriter. Figure out what you are good at and then capitalize on it. Look for ways to add value to your services. When you shop for your cable packages you often see various plans you can choose from. In those plans, they offer specialty networks like Showtime, or HBO family and depending on what you like, or need will determine what you will add to your package. Do you see what just happened? The cable company not only got your business, but they presented you will option's that catered to what you liked.

Bundling is the same way you can increase each customer transaction by adding value or adding to what you already offer. Create extras and do it based on what you know people will like in your line of business.

*I will find ways to increase my value and enlarge my coast!*

**Incorporate a new practice or procedure**

Have you ever been at a job where you get the same complaint from customers repeatedly, and you wonder why the company won't change the process or procedure? Well, people are wondering the same thing about you. New practices attract new business and new procedure correct deficiencies in your business. Finding new ways to enhance your business is a must. You are your biggest promoter. No one can promote you like you can. Maybe start an email campaign, attend a trade show in your industry to get fresh ideas. Take time out to see what's trending or pose questions on social media to get feedback.

If you are a career seeker, this is also a good practice when presenting yourself to employers. Look at what you have been offering and fine tune your process. Change up your resume or add accounts like LinkedIn to interact with recruiters. Give people a business view and not a personal view of who you are, because people will use the social you to judge how professional you are and what you can bring to the table. We all want to unwind and be social without being judged, but if you only present yourself one way then that will be all they have to judge you on. Keep your personal pages private and be careful who you befriend, this can make the difference in your professional career or business relationships.

Depending on whether you are an entrepreneur, or you have a small staff under you. Brainstorming is always good, and it has been around since the 1950s. Even though it has been around a long time, you can still use it to come up with creative, fresh ideas. Fresh ideas can open doors to more business and a higher return. Anything you do can benefit from a brainstorming session. Brainstorming is the key to innovation and should be done not only in business but career planning. Here are a few brainstorming techniques:

Reverse brainstorming, with reverse brainstorming you don't come up with resolutions. You find ways to create more problems. How does this help? When you come up with ways to make things worse, it helps you figure out how to improve your situation. It also allows you to brainstorm in a way that most people are not used to. You will be surprised at how many good things come out of finding the worst-case scenarios.

Collaborative brainstorming, collaborative brainstorming is group brainstorming with those of like mind. Collaborating is when you meet with various people in your same field or within your organization and come up with ideas to improve your business.

Individual brainstorming, individual brainstorming is when you take your ideas and put them down on paper or in a tablet to compile a group of ideas you can choose from. Individual brainstorming can also use a role technique where you put yourself in someone else's shoes and ask yourself what they would do. For example, what would Steven Jobs do or any significant person or mentor you may look up to do in a specific situation.

By using any of these three brainstorming methods, you must be open to failed and successful ideas. The point of brainstorming is to be innovative and get your creative juices flowing in an open free flowing way.

*I will no longer be afraid to take a risk and try new things!*

**Find ways to compete in the market and offer what your competition is not?**

Competition does not have to be cutthroat and is better when you can shake hands in the end. Know what you are offering and make sure it is of quality and integrity. Sometimes it is a good idea to go to your competition's business and see how they operate. In doing this, you can visualize some things that you may or may not want for your business. It does not hurt to shop around. This will also help your creative juices to flow. Healthy competition in business keeps people honest, it gives customers options, and it makes business owners stay accountable. When we lose competition in business, we start to see poor service and higher prices. So, don't be the business that takes advantage of people. Know what you are offering and make sure it is of quality and integrity.

A lot of times we don't offer something different from the competition, we become a carbon copy, and customers then view you based on factors that may not be business related. For example, you walk into any beauty supply store, and it's often overcrowded with beauty supplies and hair. They all look and feel the same. When we see carbon copy businesses how do consumers decide who to support? Consumers then judge you on your attitude, where you are located, your price structure. Apart from the price, this is not how you want your customers or clients to make decisions when it comes to supporting your business.

You may even review your competitor's customer reviews to see what they are doing well and what they are doing wrong. You may even see things you are doing that are not favorable to your customers, being done by others. When you start to look at what others are doing in your industry, you can come up with creative ways to help your business stand out. The idea here is to avoid becoming a "carbon copy" and create a new and exciting experience that only your business or services will provide.

*I will create the (fill in your name) experience for each customer, personal event or client!*

### The Follow-up

Always show gratitude to and for your customers. They are your roadmap for more customers. Follow-up is especially crucial when you need feedback on a new product or service. Everyone likes to feel appreciated, and the benefit of following up allows you to make improvements for the next customer. A great follow up tool is Facebook and your website. You can make your business page an interactive tool for feedback, group discussions, and small focus groups.

Let's say you are an author and you have a book signing. You want people to share your book, but you also want to create a buzz. Use these tools to your advantage by creating live sessions with the author to get feedback on what people thought about your book. This is an interactive way to get more people involved and to have the meet and greets online. This allows you to have a broader audience and build up the anticipation.

Another cool way people use live sessions is hairdressers and barbers doing live customer sessions online. People love to see how well you work and how you can transform your customers right before their eyes. You would be surprised at how often these videos are shared and doing short tutorials, or product review are also great ways to interact with the public.

Another way to follow up is to check reviews. Always look at how satisfied people are and how you can rectify their concerns. People may have bad experiences with you but it all in how you address the experience that makes the difference. Not only do you remedy the situation with the disgruntled client, but you also let others see how you handle issues and that you are approachable and concerned about customer satisfaction.

Never use a follow up as an opportunity to bash or argue with a customer. If you see an issue arising, choose a different method to communicate. You don't want to create a bad experience for all your followers because you can't control a customer's behavior. Politely apologize and offer a phone call or personal email to resolve intractable disputes.

*I will be a servant leader!*

# CHAPTER THREE

*"While men inhabiting different parts of this vast continent cannot be expected to hold the same opinions, they can unite in a common objective and sustain common principles."*

*~ Franklin Pierce*

# Chapter 3 – Marketing is key- Go viral

In your daily planning, we will talk more about planning in the next chapter; you want to take an hour and explore trending topics, news stories, and viral videos. Learning what is trending will help you grow your business and expand your market. Marketing is a massive focus for any business so finding the best tools to use, keeping up with your field and monitoring what you put out is key to a successful marketing campaign. Going viral is not only the new trend, but it can take you from a mom and pop shop to an international sensation in a matter of minutes. So how do people go viral?

**Best tools for going viral**

Going viral is a marketing dream for any business or individual who wants to be noticed. Finding out the methods of going viral is easy but going viral can be tricky because it's controlled by the population's desire to share your information at a rapid pace.

Here are a few ways to help facilitate a viral experience for your business:

1) Build a following through email, social media and in your local community to showcase your brand.
2) Look for ways to be guest featured on popular websites, with popular bloggers, or with complementary businesses. Tie what you do with other trending and viral topics.
3) Use search engine marketing or pay per click ad options to get noticed on the worldwide web, and

4) Target popular search terms, words, and phrases, so people find you. Once people can locate you give them great content that keeps them coming back for more. People love tutorials, product reviews, and hearing from an expert who knows their stuff.

**Keep up with what is going on in your field**

This involves checking for new updates in your field such as salary outlooks, new tools or new education requirements. People in the medical profession are an excellent example of a career that requires constant learning, CME conferences, and new pharmaceutical reviewing. Also, in Real Estate agents must take continuing education courses bi-annually to learn about new laws and refresh themselves on existing laws. Sometimes you may have to take extra classes to keep up with the competition or expand your level of knowledge. For example, becoming a broker in real estate requires additional education, but it is an advanced option or an opportunity to start your own firm. Ultimately the more you know, the bigger your business will grow. Simply renewing your mind can open new windows of opportunity to you and spark ideas of entrepreneurship. Don't limit yourself even if you have a specific career you can still venture out and seek additional opportunities.

***I will not be a follower but a leader that knows my field of expertise and offers more than the norm!***

**Check your sites and monitor as if you were a customer**

This is my biggest pet peeve with business owners. When your website is up and running, you should view it as a customer would. What looks useful to you? What appeals to your senses? What would you change? What would you add?

The most significant thing you are looking for is errors. Misspelled words, wrong addresses, price information that is outdated or another business showing up at your address. Now that's the worse! This applies to any marketing materials you have that are visible to your customers or the public.

True story, I'm heading home from work, and I decide I want to get my hair done. I am one of those customers that hates to wait, likes reasonable rates and excellent service. I have two places I normally go, so if one doesn't answer the other one will. Now I know you heard that line before. So, anyway, back to the story. I decide to call one salon no answer, so that means my business is now going to salon B. Now salon B I'm still feeling out, so I don't have the number saved. I then pull google to search them out. Google dials the salon and guess what it's the wrong number. So, I go to Salon B's Facebook page same wrong number. So now I'm a little irritated because this salon has been in business a few years. So, my question now to the business owner is how often do you look at your business Facebook page or other social media accounts for reviews and accuracy? I tell this story because the business lost a sale because of this single error. Things like this can cause extreme lost in business depending on the services you provide.

**Come up with three different marketing plans that will help you grow**

Marketing plans consist of trying to see what will increase your business or add value to your brand. The key thing is finding something about yourself to market. Are you pleasing to the eye, do you have cute kids or adorable pets? What can you do to create a brand and create a buzz using what God gave you. "You" are your direct free resource provided by God. Next, find out what audience your business caters to. Do surveys or polls to see what people in your market want? Survey what they are missing in the market. Lastly, let your third marketing plan consist of physical materials. One option may be passing out flyers or consistently updating your social media advertisements.

The second option may be giveaways or offer Groupon's. In a coupon society filled with social media, you can get very creative with advertising your business, and you can do it on any budget. Check out the advertising platforms on Facebook; you will find options that allow you to run a small ad budget weekly or monthly and this is just one example.

Business cards are also a great way to connect with people. Business cards give you the opportunity to approach people, start conversations, and create opportunities. Business cards make anyone approachable, and you never know what's in store once your card changes hands or leaves a business counter. My very first listing appointment came from a stack of business cards I left on the counter at a diner. After you do your initial marketing plans and put things into action the measuring stick is how people respond. If the response is slow don't fret, sometimes it may take a little longer for people to catch on but keep the momentum high and the marketing going.

*Marketing is the best form of flattery; I will find ways to share my passion with the world!*

# CHAPTER FOUR

*"The essence of knowledge is, having it, to apply it; not having it, to confess your ignorance."*

*~ Confucius*

# Chapter 4- Knowledge

Learning is the key to growing everything you do in life. We learn how to eat, walk, and talk when we are young, and as adults, we learn how to continue to eat, how to walk into our destinies, and how to talk to and communicate with people in a way that makes people admire us and respect us. Knowledge is what separates you from being a dreamer. The more you know about anything, the better you are at putting it into action. We learn from friends, business associates, books, blogs and even social media platforms. Every moment we take in life to learn will benefit us. Just be sure you learn from factual sources and take other sources like a grain of salt. There is a learning opportunity in everything we encounter just be wise about what you apply to your life. Also, keep in mind learning has no barriers. Age, skin color, or social status is never a barrier to learning.

**Seek change and incorporate new ideas**

Many business owners and entrepreneurs that have been in business for a few years will tell you, "I've been doing this the same way since I started" or "If it ain't broke don't fix it." Wrong! These are the same people who are working themselves to death, not employing others because they cannot afford it, and maintaining the same small customer base year after year. They have not broken out of a cycle of the same process, same services, and same prices. To grow, you must be open to change. Businesses must evolve with the time and seek out what's trending. You do not have to follow every trend but always be open to what people are asking for, after all, you are in business for them, not to be your own customer.

Reading about new techniques or blogs in your field is very beneficial to your business needs. This also includes reading up on ways to improve your business, basically what you are doing right now. I always find myself seeking out articles on topics that will help me in my line of work or about new innovative ideas and products. Learning increases your knowledge and is favorable to your growth. The knowledge obtained can be shared with others in a motivational or life-changing way.

**Seek out a Coach or Mentor**

Having a business coach or mentor does not hurt; it enhances and adds value to your profession and your vision. They can be especially helpful when you are starting out in business. There are many people who open businesses because they possess a skill, but they don't know the first thing about business. Skills draw in the business and knowledge of business helps keep you open and busy.  Have you ever seen a business or a store and wonder how do they stay open because no one is ever in there? Envision one place packed every day and another place with the same services empty. Have you ever wondered why customers choose the crowded service provider over the empty one? Is the difference your business knowledge or your direct skills? Undoubtedly, skills don't keep your business afloat if you have poor customer service, overpriced services, and a lack of advertisement. Having a business consultant, coach or mentor can help grow your business, enhance your skills, and give you dos and don'ts of how a business should run. They also give you pointers on how to increase revenue, meet legal requirements and face unforeseen obstacles. Consultants can look at your overall structure and plan and make the proper assessments to tweak your business structure for the better. A coach will help keep you motivated and energized because being a professional is not as easy as it looks.

## Take Retreats as a group and Network

This covers all types of business professionals. It gives you an outlet but also serves as a platform for learning and knowledge growth in business. We all need rest and relaxation. If you work for yourself, or a company, always make sure to take time out to recuperate, regroup, and refocus. This gives you a chance to refresh yourself and produce new ideas. If you have a team of employees, they can help you produce new ideas and concepts while on fun retreats. It also gives your team a chance to relax and have a creative outlet for ideas.

Networking is also a great social business tool; it is a business event with a social vibe that gives you access to new business to business relationships. Instead of looking for the next club outing with friends try some business networking and group retreats. Once you start attending these retreats, you will look forward to the to refresh. When starting out on a small scale seek out local networking events. Also, try groups on social media where you can network with like-minded individuals.

*Good company helps spark great ideas!*

## CHAPTER FIVE

*"Be fit for more than the thing you are now doing. Let everyone know that you have a reserve in yourself; that you have more power than you are now using. If you are not too large for the place you occupy, you are too small for it."*

~ *Chester A. Arthur*

# Chapter 5 – Lifestyle business

In business and career, we can be versatile. We don't have to fit the mold of other career seekers and business owners. Having a combination of mini business ventures and a career can also be beneficial to many. Especially people who are blessed with many talents. When you have multiple talents, you don't want to hide them, or you will see more lost than gain over your lifetime. Begin your journey by looking at niche opportunities. How many people want an extra 100,000.00 a year? Well, a niche business can afford you that and more. For example, a beauty blog can earn you an additional 500.00 a month. Whatever you do well and have a passion for can make you extra money. The key to starting a lifestyle business is meeting a need and doing it with minimal effort. We all have niche skills and a gift that we are not using. When we utilize all our gifts, we can ignite a fire that will burn in many places and not just one single spark that may one day burn out.

**What is a Lifestyle business?**

Lifestyle businesses are small businesses that you can manage while maintaining a fulltime job or a school schedule. People can also operate two or three lifestyle businesses without stretching themselves to thin. When seeking lifestyle business opportunities, you want to find options that do not require constant attention. The idea is to have a business that can run with minimal guidance. Having a niche is also important in lifestyle businesses because it allows you to focus in on one thing. Going back to blogging, this is an example of a lifestyle business. You can write about things that interest you and draw advertisers to your blog that pay you for attracting readers.

### Where do I find ideas for Lifestyle businesses?

The internet has a wealth of information on resources for starting any type of lifestyle business and examples of people who have made lots of money in the process. The key to having these types of business is to have a focus or niche. Poll your community of friends on social media to see what is in high demand. Find out what products you can offer that will either fill a need or meet a demand. If you are writing a book, take on topics that are relevant to the times. Many people may be seeking guidance in a specific area or looking to learn from the experiences of others. No matter what you choose, do not try to take on 100 things at once the key here is to focus on one thing at a time. With a more niche business focus, even career seekers can seek out entrepreneurial opportunities without struggling for time or money. Even if you're in MLM try to have a focus, there are hundreds of people selling the same product but find out how you can stand out and how you can create a specialized service in an MLM market.

### Knock and doors shall open

Seeking opportunity is the only way to get through the door. Some people sit back and wait for an opportunity to fall from the sky. I need a job. I do not know my purpose. What will I do with my life? These are the questions many career seekers and potential business owners are asking. The question is, are you seeking a job. Are you beating down the doors to find your purpose? What are you doing with your life besides wondering what to do with your life? Once the mindset changes and you start to seek out opportunities, then you will see a shift in business opportunities and doors that open to you. Never giving up is the key to success. We do not always achieve what we want on our timetable, and many times this is because our path is predestined. When we take that into consideration, we may be making our path more difficult every time we insist on our way of doing things. How do we avoid these pitfalls?

1. Follow your heart and your dreams

2. Listen to those who have come before you, being sure they are guiding you in the right direction

3. When doors close do not get upset, it just means a better opportunity awaits you

4. Finish what you start

**Venturing out from a fulltime job**

Once you graduate and find your dream job, does it allow you to do everything you set out to do? Can you pay all your bills? Are you able to afford your student loans? Did your quality of life improve or are you still living paycheck to paycheck? Many people will not be able to travel and eat out at expensive restaurants because bills have taken over once the job starts. This is where venturing out and starting lifestyle businesses can be beneficial. You can focus on a specific task like paying off a massive debt or taking annual vacations. Making one of your significant obligations or the desired trip the focal point allows you to have two goals completed at once. Whatever your end goal is don't let having a single income limit your potential. Look at the most successful people in the world. Do they just do one thing? No, of course not. So why do we focus on one job, one income, and decide it should take care of all our needs and when it doesn't. Why live a poor unfulfilled life when you can live exponentially?

*Don't let your means be your end!*

# CHAPTER SIX

*"A True leader leads by decreasing their presence on the front line and being exalted through the excellence of the people they serve."*

# Chapter 6 – Become the CEO

## Find ways to move up in your own company or career

If you are the sole owner of your company, then you are already the CEO. As your company grows, you will have to hire people to work for you, and if you don't, you will just be your own employee, not the CEO. The CEO should be able to trust others to manage and run their business while maintaining the values you have set for your company. If you are at a point where you cannot trust anyone to work on your behalf or manage work within your business, then you are not running the business, again you are simply your own employee.

If you are an employee, you need to seek out new opportunities and ways to advance. If you are ever in a position where you reach the ceiling, then you can look at adding certifications, more education, or look for shadowing opportunities with others in your company to gain new skills. There are always opportunities to advance even if it's a new company. Never be afraid to venture out and seek new opportunities. If you are newly hired, then research the Occupational Labor book or other online resources for the salary of your position and be sure to take in consideration your location and the cost of living when doing so.

Then choose your salary based on a range, your education level, and experience. This can be extremely helpful coming out of school and being new to the job market.

## Give yourself a raise

As a business owner, you will find that you get paid last and sometimes the least when starting out. You also work far more hours than you would on a normal 40 hour a week job.

When you consider all these things, you may be making minimum wage or just breaking even when you factor in your overhead and other business expenses. How can you avoid these pitfalls and make being a business owner work for you versus against you? First, make it a goal annually to pay yourself a little more each year. Even if the increase is small, this will motivate you to continue to improve your business and encourage growth.

The goal is to have CEO status not only as a title but also in compensation. One way to do this is to monitor your hours worked. This is extremely important and takes skill and focus. You want your business to work, but you don't want to burn yourself out and work more than you earn in the process. Part of this comes from properly planning and scheduling. Each week take an assessment of hours worked, and monies earned. After you have these figures, calculate what time was wasted and how you were most effective. Find ways to maximize your income vs. time wasted. Spend at least one hour looking at ways you can schedule yourself more effectively each week.

**Plan ahead**

Planning is an excellent way to reach goals, long term and short term. Previously we discussed planning for your salary, but you must also plan for your business-related events and personal time away from work. With planning, you must take time away from the hustle, and very few business owners do. Many times, we burn the candle at both ends leaving no room to plan for our next moves. One way to prepare is to buy a planner and write down your weekly goals. Another way to plan is to hire a virtual assistant who sets your schedule weekly and then sends your reminders of the plans you created the previous week.

Another planning method is a planning buddy, and this can be more cost-effective if you're just starting out.
A planning buddy is someone with a common interest or goals. It can also be a trusted employee. When planning setup weekly calls and meeting to discuss your next steps. Having a simple conversation about your plans with someone of like mind has a significant impact on how you plan from week to week. It is also fun to tell them later what you got accomplished and what you still need to work on. Make it a lunch date or a weekend get together. Whichever way you choose to be sure to stay consistent and you will see a major difference in your business life and personal life. Just don't drink too much wine during this process.

*Planning is like a fine wine, it takes time, but it's worth it in the end!*

**Train and motivate your team to be leaders**

Your team is your support group. They are there to help you grow your business. Train them. Having someone who recognizes talent in your business circle is great when it comes to this topic. When training people to be leaders, you first want to recognize who has the qualities to lead. A useful resource for finding the right people and training them is a business coach. Most coaches have a way of identifying the strengths and weaknesses of people. They are also able to assess what qualities are needed to be a leader in an industry or business setting. One technique for discovering leaders is what I like to call the blame game test. The blame game test is when you give someone a task, and you see how many times they try to blame someone else for them not being able to complete the task.

We see this all the time in retail, fast food, and other service industries someone is always looking for someone to blame when they can' t readily resolve an issue or task. Another test is a time management test. When you search for a leader to train, you want someone who manages their time well no matter what is going on. The best way to measure this is when you are not present. How does your employee manage their time when you are not round? After you test for potential leaders, you want to increase their task by allowing them to run a department meeting or train another employee. Training and motivating others to lead is a great way to prepare for the move into CEO status, as we discussed earlier.

# CHAPTER SEVEN

*"Nothing can stop the man with the right mental attitude from achieving his goal; nothing on earth can help the man with the wrong mental attitude."*

*~ Thomas Jefferson*

# Chapter 7-Surviving the Grind

Business is a daily grind no matter what you do. Whether you work for a corporation or you, run a boutique. You wake up with business on your mind, and you go to sleep with business on your mind. Surviving the daily grind is key to success in anything you do.

**Daily restoration techniques**

Here are simple things you can do to keep a level head in a world where everything is going 90 miles per hour when you just need a moment to recuperate. To stay motivated, you must restore yourself with these day-to-day practices.

1. Take a walk

Walking helps you not only exercise, but it gives you a freeing moment to let your mind rest and let your thoughts wander. The motion of walking is needed for your mind and body.

2. Stay Hydrated

When you drink water, you not only hydrate your body, but you also think more clearly. Water sends oxygen to your brain and helps your entire system. When you are hydrated, you can think, communicate, and focus. In business concentration and focus is key to producing great ideas.

3. Meditate

Taking ten to twenty mins of day to meditate helps you clear your thoughts and breathe. It also gives you an opportunity to connect spiritually. Meditation is a great way to step away from the dull or crazy moments that arise in a business day.

4. End your day

Learn to end your day. Don't take work home. It's okay to discuss your day but don't let it consume home and personal life. Make sure you give your personal life the attention it needs. Spend family time and don't neglect your significant other for work that will be in the same place you left it.

5. Rest

You can't survive without sleep. Many times, we think we need to work night and day to be successful. If you work night and day, you open yourself up to vices, and you put so much stress on your body that it will eventually break down. So, no matter how much you have going on get the proper rest, so you keep grinding for another day. Relaxation is a key component to a healthy you.

6. Enjoy your spoils

The reason you work and maintain your business is to support yourself. You work hard, and therefore you should also enjoy the money you make. Even if you are just starting out treat yourself to something small every week. No one wants to grind in business just to pay bills. The reward should be sweet.

7. Give back

Giving produces a great feeling, and it is the extra mile you can go for all your hard work. Giving is the most selfless thing you can do because of your hard work. It is also giving you the most significant reward and a feeling of calm. When you are giving cheerfully, you will find yourself gaining more, and it often results in a sense of peace in all you do. Don't ever be afraid to give, trust the process and you will see results in everything you do.

**Setting Goals**

You always want to set goals in your life. You probably set more goals that you are aware of. When you were little, you had goals to go outside or get good grades. No matter had big or small it was something you planned, set your mind to, and executed. Now think back over your life at every goal you set big or small. You could write several pages filled with all the goals you set in life. Now think about the goals you set in the last five years. How many have you accomplished? Why is it that the older we get, the harder it becomes to complete our goals? Well, life gets in the way and all the people we encounter in life help us push our goals off, including those people we love the most. How we manage the goals that we set is the key to accomplishing them.

**Life and business affirmations**

Every day speak life into your business and career goals. For the next thirty days take the time to start your day with an affirmation that will help you improve your spirit. When you are happy, driven, and encouraged you to accomplish more. Remembering that you have a purpose and giving yourself a daily affirmation before you start your day or at the end of your day will not only increase your drive, but it will refresh you after you go through the fire. Also, do not hesitate to repeat the affirmations every thirty days.

## DAILY AFFIRMATIONS

### Day 1

I am here for a purpose, and today I will seek my purpose.

### Day 2

I am going to win!

### Day 3

I am creative in my own way; today I will explore my creative side or creative connections.

### Day 4

I am a brand; today I will focus on what my brand is and how I will showcase me.

### Day 5

I will keep pushing forward, no weapon formed against me shall prosper.

## Day 6

I am stronger than I think, I will survive the day!

## Day 7

I can make a difference in this world starting today.

## Day 8

I am on a mission, and today I will achieve a goal.

## Day 9

I am even more powerful when I seek knowledge.

## Day 10

I will only focus on the positive aspects of today.

## Day 11

I will learn from my mistakes and overcome them.

## Day 12

I will not be defeated; my business will succeed.

### Day 13

I will smile today and be a blessing!

### Day 14

I will remove negativity from my life.

### Day 15

I am open to proper guidance today.

### Day 16

I am a vessel of knowledge and Knowledge I shall seek.

### Day 17

My character is strong, and I am confident.

### Day 18

I am above and not beneath.

### Day 19

My steps are ordered, I will not be led astray.

### Day 20

I am wonderfully and fearfully made!

### Day 21

I am following the plan today, no detours.

### Day 22

I am a successful businessman/ woman.

### Day 23

I am worthy!

### Day 24

I am the lender and not the borrower.

### Day 25

I am positive and hate free!

### Day 26

I am a seeker of good works.

## Day 27

I am walking in my purpose!

## Day 28

I am great, and I have wonderful things to offer.

## Day 29

I am producing new strategies today.

## Day 30

I am proud of me,

I am blessed and focused!

*Prepare your work outside; get everything ready for yourself in the field, and after that build your house.*

*Proverbs 24:27*

### Let's recap your mission

The ultimate message in business and life is to prepare. Go out and prepare yourself for the challenges ahead. Next get ready, you must get ready to receive everything you have prayed for and prepared for. Lastly build, now that you have done the work you can start to build the foundation and then live in what you have created. Set boundaries, order and be open to receive instruction as you move into your purpose as a business owner, a career-driven individual and or an entrepreneur. As business professionals, we want to take inventory of our business and personal lives to ensure we are still in line with our goals and our purpose. We want to create heirs and live a rich life. For everyone, the rich life is different and not based on your net worth but on your happiness. By implementing all the practices discussed in this book, the business of day to day life can also run smoother. Apply these tips to any business arrangements you have. The business of kids, marriages, relationships and even school. This way you are prepared for work, and company challenges.

The tool given in this book will ultimately help you build, change and grow. Do not be afraid to seek other tools and use other resources that you have around you as well. The idea here is to stay driven and not get so far off course that we cannot rescue ourselves, our businesses, or our careers. This is the year that you implement all these tools. Assess your current situation to be sure you are leading a balanced life that allows you to be focused. You must give yourself a S.M.A.C.K, every time you lose focus or steer away from your goals.

**Strategize**, learn techniques where you can build and find new ways of doing business.

**Marketing**, always key in on ways to market yourself and business. This is very important because marketing gets your brand noticed.

**Act**, action is key to driving the business. Everything is related to the favorable actions you put in motion and If you fail to act your business will suffer.

**Create**, tap into the creativity of others as well as your own creativity. When we create new innovative ideas, we can only go up.

**Knowledge**, seek out all avenues of learning, whether it is reading books or taking classes. Education will always help you advance up in your career and give you tools to use in your business. It also gives you time to reorganize your business goals.

Lastly, encourage yourself to keep going. Don't neglect the simple things that keep you going. Give yourself the daily motivation you need to prove you can do anything. One day we will all retire from the grind, and the goal is to not struggle in the retirement phases of life. In life, we sometimes forget the slowdown will come, and we must start focusing on being prepared versus struggling to keep our heads above water. Go through the building blocks laid out as many times as necessary, and you will start to see a change in how you manage the day-to-day task and business transactions. The world is changing every day So, we must keep our eyes on the prize and leave room to enjoy the fruits of our labor. Do not work so hard at the business that you lose sight of your purpose. Business is Business, after all.

*This may be the end of the book but its the beginning for YOU!*

*So let your business be about business because BUSINESS IS BUSINESS!*

www.ingramcontent.com/pod-product-compliance
Lightning Source LLC
Chambersburg PA
CBHW040241220526
45473CB00001B/319